CONTENTS

Pumpkin Dog Biscuits
Easy No Bake Soft Cookies
Christmas Star Cookies
Delicious Dog Cookies
No Bake Snowball Treats
Minty Stars
Peanut Butter Pralines
Stuffed Christmas Apples
Gingerbread Cookies
No Bake Golden Truffles
Crunchy Carob Biscuits
Carob Chip Cookies
Delicious Soft Cakes
Easy Carrot Cupcakes
Fruity Biscuits
Christmas Gummies
Doggy Donuts
Sweet Potato Pralines
Easiest Cookies Ever
Banana Meringues

CONTENTS

General Tips & Tricks
Decorating Tips & Tricks

Pumpkin Dog Biscutis

How to do it:

Preheat oven to 350F(175C)

Put all ingredients in one bowl and mix them until you get fine dough.

Place the dough on flat surface and use your rolling pin to make it flat and thin.

Use the cookie cutter to cut desired shapes.

Bake at 350F (175C) for 35 - 40 minutes.

Wait till completely cool before decorating.

Ingredients

- 2 Tablespoons Peanut butter (xylitol free)
- 2 Eggs
- 2+1/2 Cups Whole wheat flour
- 1/2 Teaspoon cinnamon
- 1/2 Cup canned pumpkin
- 1 Teaspoon Baking soda

Tips - Tricks - Notes

Pumpkin is great for anal gland problems.

Easy No Bake Soft Cookies

How to do it:

Put all ingredients in one bowl.

Use spoon or fork to combine ingredients then use your hands to form a dough.

Create small (or biger) balls and flatten them with your hand to make a cookie.

You can wrap the dough around piece of cheese for super delicious treat.

Ingredients

1 Cup Quick oats

1 Cup Peanut butter (xylitol free)

1/3 Cup Chicken broth

Tips - Tricks - Notes

These soft cookies are great for when you need to hide a pill.

Christmas Star Cookies

How to do it:

Preheat oven to 350F(175C)

Put eggs, oil and honey in a bowl and whisk well.

Add flour and mix till you get fine dough.

Place the dough on flat surface and use your rolling pin to make it flat and thin.

Use the cookie cutter to cut stars.

Bake until golden, for approximately 15 minutes.

Wait till completely cool before decorating.

Ingredients

1+1/4 Cups Flour

2 Eggs

2 Tablespoons Canola oil

1 Tablespoon Honey

Tips - Tricks - Notes

You can use any vegetable oil, but canola oil is great for maintaining healthy skin and coat

Delicious Dog Cookies

How to do it:

Preheat oven to 350F(175C)

Put all ingredients in one bowl and mix them until you get soft dough. If dough is too dry add few drops of water.

Place the dough on flat surface and use your rolling pin to make it flat and thin (about 1/4" - 0.5 cm).

Use the cookie cutter to cut desired shapes.

Bake at 350F (175C) for 15 minutes or until golden.

Wait till completely cool before decorating.

Ingredients

2 Cups Flour

1 Cup Peanut butter (xylitol free)

1 Cup Plain Greek yogurt

1 Tablespoon Baking powder

Water

Tips - Tricks - Notes

Whole wheat flour is always the best choice when making dog treats.

No Bake Snowball Treats

How to do it:

Put coconut oil, peanut butter and oats in one bowl or food processor.

Mix until well combined.

Skoop small amount of mixture with a spoon and roll into small balls.

Roll each ball in shredded coconut until fully coated.

Refrigerate for at least 30 minutes before serving.

Ingredients

1/3 Cup Coconut oil
3 Tablespoons Peanut butter (xylitol free)
2+1/2 Cups Rolled oats
1/3 Cup Shredded coconut

Tips - Tricks - Notes

Coconut oil has natural antiviral, antibacterial, and anti-fungal properties

Minty Stars

How to do it:

Preheat oven to 350F(175C)

Put all ingredients in one bowl and mix them until you get fine dough. If dough is too dry add more water and if it's too wet add some more shredded coconut.

Place the dough on flat surface and use your rolling pin to make it flat and thin (about 1/4" - 0.5 cm).

You can sprinkle some coconut on the surface to make it less sticky.
Use the cookie cutter to cut desired shapes.

Bake at 350F (175C) for 15 minutes on one side and 15 on the other.

Leave to cool in the oven.

Ingredients

- 2 Cups Flour
- 4 Tablespoons Finely shredded coconut
- 1 Tablespoon Coconut oil
- 4 Tablespoons Chopped fresh mint
- 1 Cup Water

Tips - Tricks - Notes

Mint's a good source of vitamins A and C and dogs love it.

Peanut Butter Pralines

How to do it:

Put all ingredients in a double boiler pot on stove.

Stir until mixture is completely melted and well combined.

Pour mixture into bite size silicone molds.

Chill treats in refrigerator until they're hard.

Ingredients

1 Cup Peanut butter (xylitol free)
1 Cup Coconut oil
1 Teaspoon Cinnamon

Tips - Tricks - Notes

Peanut butter is a wonderful source of protein and healthy fat for your dog.

Stuffed Christmas Apples

How to do it:

Wash and core the apple using aple corer.

Make sure aple is completely cored and seeds free.

Put peanut butter with coconut and cinnamon in a cup and mix with spoon until well combined.

Fill the apple and let cool for 30 minutes.

Ingredients

- 1 Apple
- 1 Tablespoon Peanut butter (xylitol free)
- 1 Teaspoon Finely shredded coconut
- Pinch of cinnamon

Tips - Tricks - Notes

This treat is great substitute for kong and your dog will love it.

Gingerbread Cookies

How to do it:

Preheat oven to 350F (175C)

Whisk egg, honey, applesauce, ginger and cinnamon in a bowl.

Add flour and knead to form a dough.
If the dough is too dry, add water one tablespoon at a time.

Place the dough on flat surface and use your rolling pin to make it flat and thin (about 1/4" - 0.5 cm).

Use the cookie cutter or knife to cut small gingerbread men.

Bake at 350F (175C) for 25 minutes or until golden brown.

Wait till completely cool before decorating.

Ingredients

- 2 Cups Flour
- 1 Egg
- 1 Tablespoon Finely chopped fresh ginger
- 2 Tablespoons Honey
- 1/2 Cup Applesauce
- Pinch of Cinnamon

Tips - Tricks - Notes

Ginger is great natural heartworm treatment alternative.

No Bake Golden Truffles

How to do it:

Whisk the yogurt and peanut butter until you get a paste.

Add pumpkin puree and mix until well combined.

Gradually add 2+1/3 cups oats.

Use spoon or small scoop to create small balls.

Roll each ball in the rest of oats.

Chill treats in refrigerator until they're firm.

Ingredients

- 1 Cup Pumpkin puree
- 1/2 Cup Peanut butter (xylitol free)
- 1/3 Cup Plain organic yogurt
- 3 Cups Rolled oats

Tips - Tricks - Notes

Pumpkin is rich in bountiful antioxidant beta-carotene which slows the aging process

Crunchy Carob Biscuits

How to do it:

Preheat oven to 350F (175C)

Mix all ingredients until you get smooth and soft dough.
If the dough is too dry, add water one tablespoon at a time.

Place the dough on flat (floured) surface and use your rolling pin to make it flat and thin (about 1/4" - 0.5 cm).

Use the cookie cutter or knife to cut desired shapes.

Bake at 350F (175C) for 10-15 minutes.

Wait till completely cool before decorating.

Ingredients

- 1 Cup Flour
- 1/2 Cup Carob powder
- 3/4 Cup Water
- 1 Teaspoon Honey
- Pinch of Cinnamon

Tips - Tricks - Notes

To make biscuits darker you can use brown rice flour instead of regular one.

Carob Chip Cookies

How to do it:

Preheat oven to 350F(175C)

Put all ingredients in a bowl and fold with spatula until you get stiff and dry dough.

Shape cookies with your hands or press the dough down onto a flat surface and cut shapes you want.

Dough will be very dry so you might want to use knife instead of cookie cuters.

Bake at 350F (175C) for 20 minutes.

Wait till completely cool before decorating.

Ingredients

2 Cups Brown rice flour
1 Cup Whole wheat flour
3/4 Cup Water
1 Teaspoon Honey
3/4 Cup Carob chips

Tips - Tricks - Notes

Carob is great and delicious source of pectin, a substance that helps to flush toxins from the body.

Delicious Soft Cakes

How to do it:

Preheat oven to 325F(160C). Brush silicone baking cups with coconut oil.

Melt the coconut oil.

Mix flour and baking powder in a large bowl. Add peanut butter, honey, oil, eggs and water.

Mix until well combined and then add the apples.

Poor the batter into cups (about 1/2 inch - 12mm in each)

Bake for 8 - 10 minutes, until the top is lightly golden brown.

When cooled decorate with frosting and sprinkles.

Ingredients

- 2 Cups Flour
- 1/2 Cup Peanut butter (xylitol free)
- 1 Teaspoon Baking powder
- 1/2 Cup Water
- 2 Teaspoons Honey
- 3 Tablespoons Coconut oil
- 2 Eggs
- 1 Cup Shredded apple (peeled)
- Silicone baking cups

Tips - Tricks - Notes

Instead of silicone baking cups you can use small baking tray.

Easy Carrot Cupcakes

How to do it:

Preheat oven to 350F(175C)

Put all ingredients in one bowl and mix until well combined.

Pour batter into lined muffin tin or baking cups.

Bake at 350F (175C) for 40-45 minutes until firm.

Once cupcakes are cooled add frosting of your choice.

Ingredients

1/2 Cup Flour
1 Tablespoon Peanut butter (xylitol free)
1/4 Cup Plain Greek yogurt
1 Teaspoon Baking powder
1 Egg
1/2 Tablespoon Honey
1/2 Cup Pumpkin Puree
1/2 Cup Shredded carrot
Pinch of cinnamon

Tips - Tricks - Notes

Add 2 tablespoons of carob chips to the batter to make cupcakes more fun.

Fruity Biscuits

How to do it:

Preheat oven to 400F(200C)

Put all ingredients in one bowl and mix and knead until you get nice non-sticky dough.

If the dough is too dry, add water 1 teaspoon at a time. If the dough is too sticky, add flour 1 tablespoon at a time.

Place the dough on flat surface and use your rolling pin to make it flat and thin (about 1/4" - 0.5cm).

Use small cookie cutters to cut desired shapes.

Bake for 25-30 minutes.

Ingredients

- 2 Cups Flour
- 1 Egg
- 1/2 Cup Chicken or beef broth
- 1/2 Cup Shredded carrot
- 1 Cup Grated apple (peeled and cored)
- 1/2 Cup Chopped cranberries
- Pinch of cinnamon

Tips - Tricks - Notes

Cranberries are rich with antioxidants that help support your dog's immune system.

Christmas Gummies

How to do it:

Mix carob powder with 1 or 2 spoons of water to get ruiny paste.

Put the rest of the liquid in the saucepan and bring to boil.

Remove from heat and let cool for 3 minutes.

Whisk in the gelatin and make sure you dissolve all clumps.

Add carrob mixture and stir to combine.

Pour mixture in molds and refrigerate for several hours.

Ingredients

1 Cup Liquid (unsweetened apple juice or water)

3 Tablespoons Plain gelatin powder

1+1/2 Tablespoons Carob powder

Pinch of cinnamon

Candy making molds

Tips - Tricks - Notes

Gelatin contains amino acids beneficial for skin, hair, and joint health.

Doggy Donuts

How to do it:

Preheat oven to 375F (190C)

Spray donut pan with cooking spray.

Put all ingredients in one bowl and mix or knead until you form a dough.

Press the dough firmly into the donut pan.

Bake at 375F (190C) for 15 minutes.

Wait till completely cool before removing donuts from the pan and decorating.

Ingredients

1 Cup Flour

1/2 Cup Peanut butter (xylitol free)

1 Cup Rolled oats

3 Tablespoons Coconut oil

2 Eggs

Pinch of cinnamon

Tips - Tricks - Notes

These donuts will not rise while baking so make sure you fill each donut cavity well.

Add chopped cranberries or carob chips for extra taste.

Sweet Potato Pralines

How to do it:

Put all ingredients ina bowl and use electric mixer to get a dough.

Fill bite size silicone molds with the mixture.

Chill treats in refrigerator until they're hard.

Ingredients

- 1/2 Cup Peanut butter (xylitol free)
- 1+1/2 Cups Crushed rolled oats
- 1 Cup Mashed sweet potato

Tips - Tricks - Notes

Sweet potatoes are one of the best dietary sources of vitamin A.

Easiest Cookies Ever

How to do it:

Preheat oven to 350F (175C)

Put flour, peanut butter and eggs in a bowl and stir to combine. Add one tablespoon of water at a time until you get fine dough.

Place the dough on flat surface and use your rolling pin to make it flat and thin (about 1/4" - 0.5 cm).

Use the cookie cutter to cut desired shapes.

Bake at 350F (175C) for 20 minutes or until golden.

Wait till completely cool before decorating.

Ingredients

2 Cups Flour

1/2 Cup Peanut butter (xylitol free)

2 Eggs

1/4 Cup Water

Tips - Tricks - Notes

Add one teaspoon of carob powder to color cookies dark.

Banana Meringues

How to do it:

Preheat oven to 350F(175C)

Use fork to mash banana in a bowl.

Add the rest of the ingredients and mix with fork or spoon until well combined.

Use teaspoon to make bite size dollops on parchment paper.

Bake for 10 minutes.

Ingredients

- 1 Egg
- 1 Cup Almond butter (unsalted)
- 1/2 Banana
- 1/2 Teaspoon Cinnamon

Tips - Tricks - Notes

You can use xylitol free peanut butter instead of almond butter.

How to do it:

INGREDIENTS

TIPS - TRICKS - NOTES

How to do it:

INGREDIENTS

TIPS - TRICKS - NOTES

How to do it:

INGREDIENTS

TIPS - TRICKS - NOTES

How to do it:

INGREDIENTS

TIPS - TRICKS - NOTES

How to do it:

INGREDIENTS

TIPS - TRICKS - NOTES

How to do it:

INGREDIENTS

TIPS - TRICKS - NOTES

How to do it:

INGREDIENTS

TIPS - TRICKS - NOTES

How to do it:

INGREDIENTS

TIPS - TRICKS - NOTES

How to do it:

INGREDIENTS

TIPS - TRICKS - NOTES

How to do it:

INGREDIENTS

TIPS - TRICKS - NOTES

How to do it:

INGREDIENTS

TIPS - TRICKS - NOTES

How to do it:

INGREDIENTS

TIPS - TRICKS - NOTES

How to do it:

Ingredients

Tips - Tricks - Notes

How to do it:

INGREDIENTS

TIPS - TRICKS - NOTES

How to do it:

INGREDIENTS

TIPS - TRICKS - NOTES

How to do it:

INGREDIENTS

TIPS - TRICKS - NOTES

How to do it:

Ingredients

Tips - Tricks - Notes

How to do it:

Ingredients

Tips - Tricks - Notes

How to do it:

INGREDIENTS

TIPS - TRICKS - NOTES

How to do it:

INGREDIENTS

TIPS - TRICKS - NOTES

How to do it:

Ingredients

Tips - Tricks - Notes

How to do it:

INGREDIENTS

TIPS - TRICKS - NOTES

How to do it:

INGREDIENTS

TIPS - TRICKS - NOTES

How to do it:

Ingredients

Tips - Tricks - Notes

How to do it:

Ingredients

Tips - Tricks - Notes

How to do it:

Ingredients

Tips - Tricks - Notes

How to do it:

INGREDIENTS

TIPS - TRICKS - NOTES

How to do it:

INGREDIENTS

TIPS - TRICKS - NOTES

General Tips & Tricks

Recipes in this book are for treats only and should NOT replace your dog's regular meals. All ingredients are perfectly safe for healthy dogs but it's always a good choice to consult your vet before introducing new food into your dog's diet.

Flour

Whole wheat flour is always better than white. For gluten free treats you can use white rice flour instead.

Dough

You can color cookie dough with all kind of natural ingredients or food colorings. If you use food colorings make sure they are 100% natural and without alcohol.

- Red: red beet powder, red raspberry puree
- Green: spinach powder
- Dark brown: carob powder
- Orange/Yellow: turmeric, carrot powder, carrot juice
- Purple/Pink: blueberries, purple sweet potato, cranberry juice, beet juice, raspberry juice

Baking

While all dog treats are good for humans too, dough is more tricky than one we normally use. Always use parchment paper or coking spray to prevent treats from sticking to the baking tray or molds.

Decorating Tips & Tricks

Shredded Coconut

You can coat treats in finely shredded coconut. Coconut can also be easily colored using natural food colorings.

Cupcake Frosting

Plain Greek yogurt or cream cheese (1 cup) and peanut butter (1 tablespoon) mixed together are great cupcake frosting.

Cookies Glaze

Mix 2 tablespoons bacon grease, chicken fat or coconut oil with 1/4 cup smooth peanut butter for delicious cookie glaze.

Sweet Icing

Mix 2 tablespoons cornstarch, 2 tablespoons water and 1 teaspoon honey and add coloring of your choice.

Carob Icing

Boil 1/2 cup water and add 1/2 cup carob powder. Stir until the mixture reaches an icing consistency.

Sprinkles

Finish decorating your treats with some sprinkles: chopped peanuts, bacon bits, sesame seeds, grated carrots, carob chips.

Printed in Great Britain
by Amazon